Building Better Therapeutic Relationships with Children

from the author

Little Windows into Art Therapy
Small Openings for Beginning Therapists
Deborah Schroder
ISBN 978 1 84310 778 1
eISBN 978 1 84642 063 4

of related interest

Motivational Interviewing for Working with Children and Families
A Practical Guide for Early Intervention and Child Protection
Donald Forrester, David Wilkins and Charlotte Whittaker
ISBN 978 1 78775 408 9
eISBN 978 1 78775 409 6

Rhythms of Relating in Children's Therapies
Connecting Creatively with Vulnerable Children
Edited by Stuart Daniel and Colwyn Trevarthen
ISBN 978 1 78592 035 6
eISBN 978 1 78450 284 3

PDA in the Therapy Room
A Clinician's Guide to Working with Children with Pathological Demand Avoidance
Raelene Dundon
ISBN 978 1 78775 347 1
eISBN 978 7 8775 348 8

BUILDING BETTER THERAPEUTIC RELATIONSHIPS WITH CHILDREN

A Creative Activity Workbook

Deborah Schroder

Jessica Kingsley Publishers
London and Philadelphia

First published in Great Britain in 2023 by Jessica Kingsley Publishers
An imprint of Hodder & Stoughton Ltd
An Hachette Company

1

Quote on page 12 is reproduced from Sommers-Flanagan &
Sommers-Flanagan, 2017 with kind permission from John Wiley & Sons.
List on page 51 is reproduced from Shannon, 2013 with kind permission from W.W. Norton.

Front cover image source: Shutterstock®. The cover image is for illustrative
purposes only, and any person featuring is a model.

Worksheet illustrations by Masha Pimas.

Disclaimer: All children's parents have granted consent or characters are composite.

A CIP catalogue record for this title is available from the British Library and the Library of Congress.

ISBN 978 1 78775 968 8
eISBN 978 1 78775 969 5

Printed and bound in the United States by Integrated Books International.

Jessica Kingsley Publishers' policy is to use papers that are natural, renewable and recyclable products
and made from wood grown in sustainable forests. The logging and manufacturing processes
are expected to conform to the environmental regulations of the country of origin.

Jessica Kingsley Publishers
Carmelite House
50 Victoria Embankment
London EC4Y 0DZ

www.jkp.com

Contents

1. Finding Joy in the Work 7

2. The Difference 16

3. Steps for Starting the Relationship 30

4. Encouraging the Adults in Our Clients' Lives 36

5. When the Issue Is Anger 44

6. My Tummy Hurts 49

7. Where Do I Belong? 58

8. Moving into Deeper Work 64

9. Connecting with Tweens 68

10. Unique Challenges 75

11. Child Clients Share Their Thoughts 85

12. Saying Goodbye 87

13. Conclusions 91

   References 94

Chapter 1

FINDING JOY IN THE WORK

Ella tenderly put her small fist in my hand and opened it, carefully depositing a small, fuzzy caterpillar in my open palm. She looked into my eyes and I knew in that moment that we were in a relationship. I gently slid Coconut the caterpillar into a small paper cup and, after Ella added some grass for him, she told me what she knew of his life story.

During her parents' separation and eventual divorce, one of the hardest issues that Ella faced was the care and feeding of her pets and creatures. Some stayed at Dad's house, some at Mom's, and Ella traveled back and forth to each home during the week.

The prior week, my initial session with Ella had been fine, a little quiet, and she warmed up enough to say that she'd come back by the end of our first session together. In this second session, the trust she gave me in letting me hold Coconut told me that we were going to do some good work together.

My own journey as a therapist has been fueled by a passion to experience a wide variety of ways of being a therapist in different settings. As an art therapist, art making has been my primary language for therapeutic interventions, and I've also played, danced, sang, learned card games and new board games and shot a lot of baskets (badly). It's quite delightful how images in art can move organically into puppetry and play.

I really like children. I state this clearly because it's so important. I've taught graduate-level students how to move into client work for many years, and when we begin to look at working with children it always feels important to me to pause and ask, "Do you like kids? What's your experience with kids?" My students know that I'm being a little playful and yet they do sense the importance of the questions. They usually laugh a little and squirm a little. And then I ask them to take turns answering those two questions.

There are plenty of other humans to help in therapy if one doesn't really like children. And children *know*. My cat can tell the moment a non-cat-person enters my home. He becomes quite watchful and wary, and refuses to be coaxed into social politeness. I think children are the same way. In my experience, if they sense a therapist is uncomfortable or stiff in relationship, their own important warning systems kick in. And, of course, if the child has been through trauma, the warning systems are always on, screening for danger. Any kind of stiff or cold beginning won't allow the warning system to be turned down even a tiny bit.

This is not to say that someone with little experience with children can't learn how to offer therapy to children. With academic and experiential preparation, and good supervision, therapists can learn how to be comfortable and therapeutic with small humans. And I still would hope that the therapist can remember how to be playful and curious, and find joy in their interactions with children.

I think it's entirely appropriate to question one's own interest in or curiosity about working with children. I spoke with my friend and colleague Teri about what some of her hesitations might be. Teri has focused on working with adults in her career as a therapist. Teri answered: "One thing that comes to mind is my own journey in childhood and how that may impact my ability to see and hear clearly. The more 'charged' the memories are the less likely I may be able to do this. I have done quite a bit of work in this area, but I admit, the thought came up for me as a possible issue" (Teri, personal communication, January 25, 2021).

The fact that Teri is willing to be curious about this seems really important. She's pausing, and approaching the idea of working with children from an honest, insightful place. People can appreciate and enjoy children and still not choose to take on the role of therapist with them.

I know my friend Teri has a playful side, but I also know adults who don't remember how to play. If you've had some good interactions with kids and enjoyed them, you're probably closer to remembering the joy of spontaneous play. From some narrative therapists who value play: "We may have sworn when we were kids that we would always remember what it was like to be a kid when we grew up. But how soon we forget. It may surprise us that we have to make a concerted effort to reclaim a knack for playful communication" (Freeman, Epston & Lobovitz, 1997, p.11).

I invite you to pause and complete Worksheet #1 in order to reconnect and perhaps get reacquainted with your childhood self.

WORKSHEET #1

Describe <u>you</u> as a child:

_____

_____

_____

_____

What did you love to do?

_____

_____

_____

_____

What didn't you like to do?

_____

_____

_____

_____

How was that? Did you remember who you were at five or eight or ten? Do you remember when you figured out that sometimes other kids liked different things than you did? I remember learning how to compromise through play. I was a girl who loved dolls, creating elaborate stories and adventures for them, and who also could be enchanted for hours drawing castles and princesses. My best friend Linda had two older brothers and she liked wilder play—using the pool table in her basement as a "bat-cave," we had a base to adventure outside from, wildly biking and saving humanity.

We will have child clients who are very different in how they are playful and creative than we remember being. The crucial thing, I think, is to remember the curiosity, magic and possibilities that perhaps were more tangible or easily accessed when we were children. I invite you to reconnect with your indoor and outdoor play memories in Worksheet #2. How did you play indoors? What was fun when you were outside?

WORKSHEET #2

what did you enjoy
doing outdoors?

_____

_____

_____

_____

_____

what did you enjoy doing indoors?

_____

_____

_____

_____

_____

_____

_____

I appreciate it if an adult voice inside you is reminding you that children are brought to therapy for serious, often very troubling or sad, reasons. I deeply believe that what we do to create a safe container for therapy to happen in is heavily influenced by how relational we as individuals seem. If my eyes, smile and willingness to have a puppet talking for me tell you that it might be safe to breathe a little and let your shoulders relax, I think we'll get to the business of therapy eventually.

I would never call myself a play therapist because I don't have that special training. I don't follow a particular theoretical protocol concerning play when I work with children. I think that what I do is playfully engage in art, storytelling, games and conversation. The power of letting my inner playfulness surface in therapy brings more to the relationship than I can adequately describe. I appreciate this thought from Fred Rogers: "It's not easy to come up with a definition of play that feels just right. And that's probably because something deep within all of us 'knows' the immense value of play" (Rogers, 1994, p.63).

How did your family think about play? In fact, what messages about childhood were shared, either spoken or unspoken, as you grew up? When I teach family therapy the discussion of spoken and unspoken rules is important to me. In the context of working with children it feels important to deeply understand the constant evolution of what childhood means to people. Many of us can still remember stories of grandparents who were plucked out of school so they could work and help support the family.

Although views on child labor have significantly changed in many places, there are definitely different views on how much responsibility children in a family should hold. How much responsibility a child holds will inform the idea of what childhood is like for that person.

We work with children whose caregivers create very different versions of childhood. And we know that external circumstances including politics, power and privilege also play a role in how caregivers create childhood, or even if they feel they have any real choices or control over what childhood feels like in their home. It can be helpful to think about your own and whether you've held onto those ideas that were present in how you were raised, or if you've intentionally thought about or offered a different experience as an adult.

It bears repeating that holding a culturally humble attitude will facilitate your ability to connect and work effectively with diverse clients... Remember to tread lightly into new cultural circumstances and remember the core principles and practices of cultural humility: Allow yourself to embrace an other-orientation, rather than focusing on your own values; hold high your respect for diverse cultural values and ways of being; and let go of any ideas you may have related to your own superiority. (Sommers-Flanagan & Sommers-Flanagan, 2017, p.470)

I had time to play as a child. I had a special place to play where my toys lived, sometimes in the basement, sometimes on an enclosed porch in the summer. This time gave me space to create the magical relationships with stuffed animals and dolls that have helped me slip into pretending and make-believe-land easily as a therapist. I invite you to reconnect with what you played with as a child in Worksheet #3.

WORKSHEET #3

Draw or describe your favorite toy:

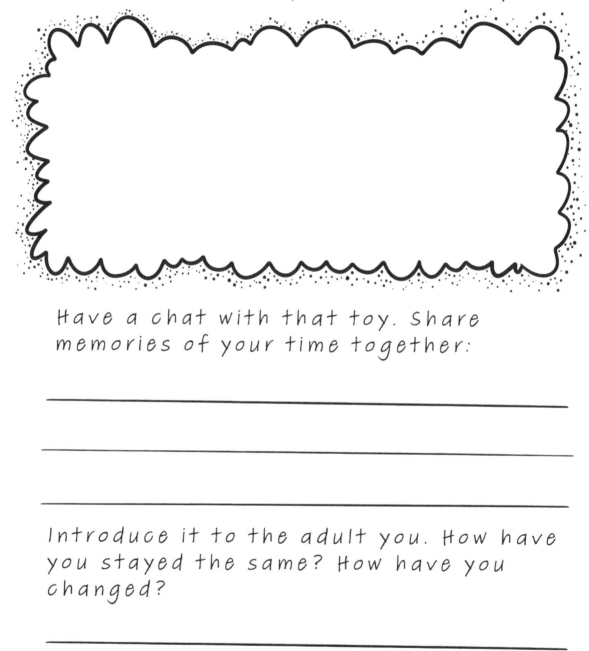

Have a chat with that toy. Share memories of your time together:

_____

_____

_____

Introduce it to the adult you. How have you stayed the same? How have you changed?

_____

_____

_____

_____

Did that help you encounter your younger self, and remember the preciousness of a relationship with a toy?

What I didn't have as a child was the freedom to be honest about my emotions. There was a belief that my siblings and I should always be "fine." So I think I bring my deep appreciation for the enormous value of sharing emotions with honesty (something I didn't experience as a child) into the therapy session as well.

And all of these experiences, as a child, as an adult, a parent, a grandparent, contribute to who I am as a therapist. I bring my own self to the work that I love. I appreciate renowned child psychotherapist Violet Oaklander's words: "We meet each other as two separate individuals, one not more superior than the other... I am as authentic as I know how to be—I am myself" (Oaklander, 2007, p.21).

Chapter 2

THE DIFFERENCE

Therapists make the decision to work with children for many different reasons. Some always knew that children would be their preferred population. Maybe they had a great time as a camp counselor or perhaps they started out as a teacher and found that they wanted a different way to impact children's lives. And some therapists started out working with adults and, because of their own interest or the needs of the community or agency, consider taking on child clients.

I get a number of phone calls from therapists who graduated from our program and need to seek guidance when making that change. Certainly it's good to seek out continuing education for therapists and also be supervised by someone who has had solid experience working with kids. And still, sometimes a therapist needs accessible, trusted advice right now! I hear things like "I just got this new job and I explained that I don't have experience with children and they still need me to start in ten days. Can you help me?"

Therapists profoundly understand that there is a difference between working with adult clients and working with children, and sometimes they only have a glimmer of how big the difference can be. This chapter looks at some of the complexities of the difference. This would be a good time to explore your thoughts and/or hesitations about working with children, using Worksheet #4.

WORKSHEET #4

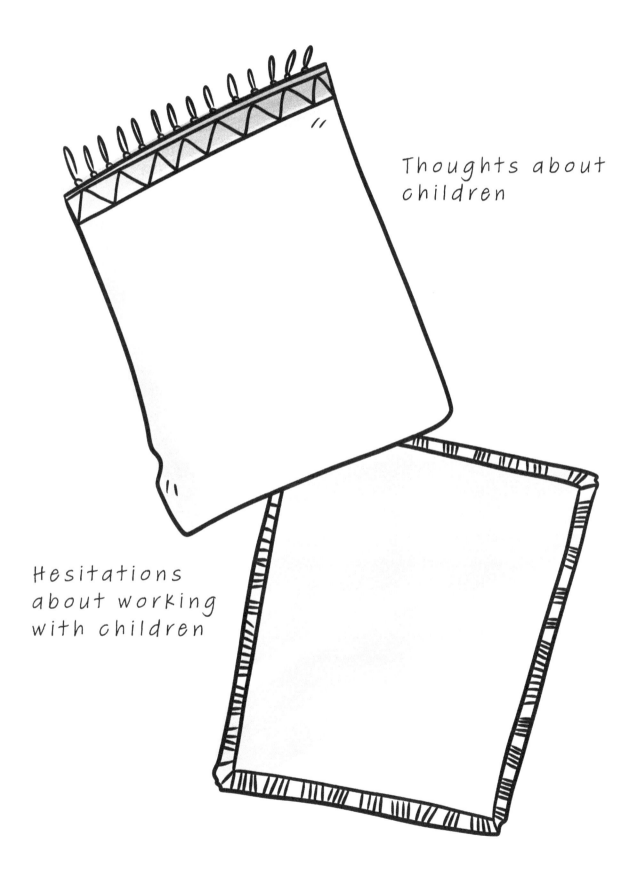

Thoughts about children

Hesitations about working with children

The question of why someone wants a child to enter therapy at the present moment, and who that person is, seems like a good beginning. External life events are often the cause of significant symptoms and unhelpful behaviors. For an adult that can be as simple as a new, demanding boss whose expectations have caused anxiety, which turns into problems with sleep, which can create mistakes and difficult relationships at work, turning into a cycle that a person can recognize as a place in life when help is needed. Children can go into a similar cycle because of an external situation, but their cycle naturally stops at that place of knowing that there could be help. Sometimes they let parents know of distress by crying or having temper problems, lashing out and misbehaving at home or school, or both. Often, children's thoughts about fixing a situation are about wanting the external issue to get taken care of rather magically. And certainly adults can cling at times to those kind of ideas—when I'm angry while driving I want the police to appear and punish the bad driver, which seems much more satisfying than me figuring out how to calm down.

So children may reluctantly be brought to therapy by a caring adult, and the therapist may be faced with difficulty from the very beginning, when faced with a small, unhappy, reluctant client. Well-known play therapist Eliana Gil spoke to this: "Children entering treatment are curious, reticent, and often anxious or afraid" (Gil, 1991, p.53). Children may be wondering how this stranger, the therapist, will help them—will they be embarrassed, will they be in trouble if they don't "do it right," what will happen?

When symptoms, behaviors or external events are more extreme, or if there is a risk to the child's health, a range of interventions and services can be considered.

Many community mental health agencies offer a variety of services, including individual child and adolescent therapy, family therapy, in-home therapy and group therapy. It is to be hoped that your role would be clearly defined as therapist, and yet there may be other responsibilities including case management, group activity leader, in-home or in-school therapist, etc. It becomes important in that setting to establish a therapeutic container for your work with individual clients. I worked for an agency serving at-risk youth and I served as kids' individual therapist, I helped watch them during lunch and recreation, I checked them in the morning for weapons and had to help intervene when there were physical confrontations. If you were my client you would experience me in many different roles, which could be confusing. So when I had an individual session I might need to say: "Today seems like it's been hard for you. And now this is your time. What do you need right now?" And we might listen to music, play a card game, whatever we needed to do in order to be in a one-to-one relationship again. Please use Worksheet #5 to define your role with your young clients.

WORKSHEET #5

What kind of role would you like to have with young clients?

How would you like to work?

Where can you imagine working?

I was honored to listen to Crystal, whom I had the pleasure of providing off-site supervision for as she worked for her independent license. I got to hear about her good work with children in two different residential treatment centers. As a therapist she provided individual and group therapy to children who needed this level of care. One site dealt primarily with children who had developmental differences, and both sites provided treatment and care for children who had been removed from their homes or foster care homes due to abuse, neglect and/or behavioral difficulties. I asked Crystal how she went about developing therapeutic relationships in those settings.

She definitely emphasized the idea of positive reinforcement. She spoke about finding the most positive thing in any encounter with a child. Sometimes that meant noticing a very tiny thing! She remembered needing to speak with a child after they'd had an emotional meltdown that had caused a disturbance on the unit, and saying to the child: "Good job! That disturbance only lasted for five minutes!" (Crystal, personal communication, February 2, 2021). She also would stop and compliment a child on their throwing arm when a child threw something at her. She had experience as a basketball player and the children must have been pleasantly surprised by what they heard in that moment.

Crystal mentioned that she really appreciated learning about "the nurtured heart" approach from a teacher at one of the sites. This approach is shared in the book *Transforming the difficult child*. In it, I especially resonated with the authors' thoughts about "Experiential Recognition" (Glasser & Easley, 1998, p.64). This concept involves the ability to notice the tiniest moments of success for a child and give clear, specific feedback for it.

Crystal noted that it seemed so easy for staff to focus on the negative in those settings. She was intentionally aware of the modeling she did through her own behavior, and the need to apologize to children when appropriate. She also was clear about giving the children power in the therapeutic relationships because they had so little control over their daily lives. She spoke about the need for adults in those settings to keep their word and follow through with plans they made with children, or with rewards.

One kind of opportunity that Crystal offered seemed especially useful in developing therapeutic relationships. She would offer the children a chance to have quiet time with her in her office while she did paperwork. They could earn this one-to-one or sometimes two-to-one privilege by their behavior, and they could choose quiet time with a game, a toy or art materials, while she worked.

Sometimes interventions required the use of breathing techniques, and all therapists usually have some they rely on, like using songs, pretending to be another creature or a phrase like "smell the roses, blow out the birthday candles." Crystal shared the idea of using peppermints to help with deep breathing. The mint sensation would help the children feel the depth of their breath. Use Worksheet #6 to note your tools for stress relief, for yourself and for your clients.

*

WORKSHEET #6

In a moment of intense stress, what do you do? In your car, at work, at home:

_____

_____

_____

_____

_____

_____

Are there things you do that could be translated to what a child could do?

_____

_____

_____

_____

_____

It was clear to me that she genuinely had fun with her young clients and found joy in those relationships. She approached each one, human to human, and I know they must have felt safe and respected with her, and genuinely liked.

Another setting where one might work with children could be in an inpatient psychiatric hospital. The role of a therapist there is very different from the role in a medical hospital, which will be discussed in Chapter 10. I worked for several years in an inpatient unit for children. The unit was quite unique in that it was able to offer extended care and children could stay there for a number of months. Today the more usual role would be working with children in terms of assessment and stabilization, and perhaps coping skills, because the length of time that the child is there might be very short. This intensifies the need for a sense of safety and the development of whatever trust is possible.

The children I worked with in that inpatient setting had deeply traumatic histories of all kinds of abuse and multiple foster homes. You can imagine how hard it was for them to trust a therapist, and their behaviors reflected how they had survived in often violent, brutal circumstances. And yet, because we had the luxury of time, we were able to develop safe, trusting relationships. I continue to turn to Bruce Perry's work for guidance and inspiration in this area:

> What maltreated and traumatized children most need is a healthy community to buffer the pain, distress and loss caused by their earlier trauma. What works to heal them is anything that increases the number and quality of a child's relationships... And, I should add, what doesn't work is well-intended but poorly trained mental health "professionals" rushing in after a traumatic event, or coercing children to "open up" or "get out their anger." (Perry & Szalavitz, 2006, p.232)

I like the idea of being one more trusted, safe person in a child's life. Perry has long been an advocate of thoughtfully building client relationships and the use of the expressive arts in therapy.

In writing about the potential for pursuing inpatient work, I'm assuming that one has the support and wisdom of a team as one grows in understanding the requirements of this kind of work. I hesitate to use the popular term "trauma-informed" because I haven't read or seen much consensus among mental health professionals about what that really means. Sometimes in outpatient work or private practice it's possible that a child is brought to therapy for a routine reason and upon exploration it turns out that a deeper trauma is underneath. Supervision and being honest about one's scope of practice is important at that point. I recommend Malchiodi's (2020) book *Trauma and expressive arts therapy*, if and when one moves forward intentionally in working with trauma.

I think that current short-term inpatient psychiatric work with children is where more therapists find positions in a psychiatric hospital setting. Assessment, stabilization and stress-reduction skills are offered by therapists and there often isn't much time for longer, deeper work. We know some things that are useful for children needing that kind of help, and first I would invite you to think about what you know that is calming and centering for you when you are faced with an extremely upsetting situation. We want to remember that on any given day, each of us can move to the disregulated place on the continuum. Take some time and use Worksheet #7 to remember your own helpful resources.

*

WORKSHEET #7

What are <u>your</u> resources for stress relief?

Activities

Practices

Interactions with humans and other creatures

Perhaps your worksheet contained a variety of options, depending on where you pictured yourself. Did you include things like walking, playing with an animal, breathing slowly, meditating, jumping, dancing, singing or breathing in lavender essence? We sometimes can forget what's available to us in the moment.

I appreciate Malchiodi's understanding of how to incorporate expressive arts in self-regulation. We know that many therapists use the well-practiced ideas associated with grounding experiences as the beginning steps toward helping clients calm themselves. That usually involves helping clients connect to the here and now by paying attention to external cues like noticing the color of the wall, the smell of the tea, the feel of an ice cube or the texture of a blanket. We know that these sensory connections help bring a person out of a disregulated state. Malchiodi described an activity that would seem especially helpful with children: "I often invite them to create something that can be used for anchoring in the present and for use outside the therapy session. For children, this can involve making a tactile object such as a stuffed toy, a painted rock, or other special object" (Malchiodi, 2020, p.169). Even in private practice I sometimes worked with children who became extremely anxious and unable to self-soothe at school, and I often had them create a soothing image, or perhaps a collage of happy, peaceful images, that they could keep in their notebook to look at as needed. Not a bad idea for adults, either. What would your happy, peaceful image be? Use Worksheet #8 to create it.

WORKSHEET #8

Please draw or use collage to create
your own happy, calm space:

I always encourage any therapist to try things out for themselves before asking a client to try it. You might put your soothing image somewhere that you can easily access it at work and see what happens. I have one for difficult, lengthy meetings!

In the context of the very time-limited setting, the simpler the tools and ideas that we share with children, the better. Simple breathing exercises that are based on a favorite cartoon character, easy tapping experiences—anything that the child could choose to do anywhere at any time—are useful. I think about stabilization in terms of what can we remind people that they already know, what can I offer that they haven't tried and what can they picture that would be helpful in the future? At this kind of site our relationships are often frustratingly fast-paced.

There are certainly other settings where we offer therapy for children that might seem more familiar to many therapists, such as private practice or shared-practice groups.

Certainly one's own space can be arranged and created in a way that feels inviting and interesting to child clients. We want to remember that our offices offer clear messages about our beliefs in terms of diversity and inclusivity. "The waiting rooms, offices, administrative offices, and general space must manifest diversity in order to welcome people of all colors and races, as well as clients who experience a sense of being marginalized or different from others" (Gil, 2021, p.43). How do we decorate our walls, so we have toys, markers and paints that speak to all skin colors? Do we have resources that are accessible and representative of everyone? "The clinician must make the playroom a safe sanctuary. Where secrecy can be shared with a trusted other" (Gil, 1991, p.195). I liked sitting at a table with clients, not at a desk. In an office that's shared with other therapists, hopefully we are able to have a closed-off cabinet space. I appreciate cabinets that close so that supplies and possibilities don't feel overwhelming. What would you want to have in your office space? How would you create a welcoming environment for everyone? Use Worksheet #9 to design your ideal space.

WORKSHEET #9

Design your ideal space:

What do you want in it?

_____

_____

_____

_____

An enormous lesson taught by the pandemic was that we could indeed create relationships with children in a very different kind of setting, through telehealth. Although it was used by therapists before the pandemic, almost everyone had to figure out how to work with children and their parents or caregivers on screen.

It actually reminded me of the in-home therapy that I used to do. Suddenly, therapists were inside clients' homes. They had to create a safe, therapeutic relationship with a child while really having no power over the things that usually help a relationship begin, like privacy, art materials, games and toys. And therapists rose to the occasion with flexibility and creativity.

Telehealth therapy with adults could still follow a somewhat recognizable pattern. Kids discovered that they could take their therapists around the house or yard by moving the screen. They could hide under the table if they didn't want to be seen, lie down on the floor, bounce around on a trampoline and turn the camera off. And sometimes Grandma would come through offering lunch, Mom or Dad could be spotted or heard in the background and pets were often part of the equation. Not all bad, but sometimes it seemed hard for therapists to really have quality, confidential time with their young clients.

The young clients often seemed much more at ease with the technology at hand. "Since technology is the facilitator of modern children's playing and communication, it is imperative to determine how it could be welcomed into treatment" (Altvater, 2021, p.173).

I try to encourage therapists to hold onto some common-sense rules that they can negotiate with their very young client and the adult who's present, from the start. The more we treat the screen like the therapy office, the easier this all will go. Confidentiality is important: where can the child be, and will adults, siblings and other relatives respect the need for privacy?

Having your own toys present can help. Perhaps your favorite puppet or toy could talk with your client's favorite toy as a way to begin the relationship, and the adult in the room could step back.

Simple things, like sticking to the appointment time, wearing clothes appropriate for a therapy session, and using materials in the home for play and art making seem important.

Before trying to create a relationship with your client on screen, be sure to have a good relationship with your own available technology, and research all of those websites that offer fun backgrounds, virtual sandtrays and options for making art in the same "space" at the same time. I think it can be a fascinating balance between hearing and seeing, providing witness to your small client and having some fun using the ever-expanding world of the screen. Remember that your client is seeing your space too—does it seem inviting, somewhere a child might want to spend time in?

Chapter 3

STEPS FOR STARTING
THE RELATIONSHIP

I admit that I find it easy to feel genuine empathy for a child who seems frozen when he or she meets me for the first time. I can feel the same freeze on the inside sometimes when I meet new people, especially if we need to get a working relationship off the ground.

A child is forming her impressions of what therapy is all about even as she walks through the door. When a parent or other adult introduces the child to a therapist, she usually has little control over how she is being described, let alone an opportunity to critique or protest those descriptions. (Freeman et al., 1997, p.34)

I know that meeting someone who gives me kind or interested eye contact, has a warm smile and a friendly voice helps me feel comfortable. If someone talks fast, loud or doesn't wait for me to answer the question, I feel less comfortable and not very seen or heard. Worksheet #10 offers space to consider how you feel when meeting someone new.

WORKSHEET #10

Do you enjoy meeting new people?

_____

_____

_____

What helps you feel comfortable when you meet someone new?

_____

_____

_____

_____

Were there any adults who you liked right away when you met them?

Who and why?

After the parent or caregiver has completed paperwork and explained the reasons for bringing their child to therapy, they usually leave the room. (While they complete paperwork, there is a choice of art materials and toys present for the child.) If they don't feel comfortable leaving, or the child is quite young and needs them to stay, I introduce a simple activity that we all can participate in together, or I invite the two of them to create a picture of their favorite thing to do. As I encourage them to tell me the story of their picture, I have a chance to normalize the process by saying that this is how we'll spend time together each week, doing something together and talking. I ask if they have any questions for me. Judith Rubin spoke of establishing a consistent routine that the child can rely on: "Thus it matters that one meets with the child at a consistent place and time, that one has the same supplies available in the same locations, and that one handles routine transactions (greeting, cleaning up, leaving) in a predictable manner" (Rubin, 2005, p.61).

My friend Teri was particularly interested in knowing what first-time creative experiences I might use during an initial session. She was especially concerned about age or developmental appropriateness. I do take the idea of age and development into consideration. I also have found that although children often carry around ideas about what's "babyish or childish" to play with, they also might shift those ideas during the session if they see me playing quite happily.

I remember when William's dad got up after we'd talked, and headed to the waiting room. William was about six and I could see his big brown eyes taking in everything in the room. We sat down at a table where I had some tiny plastic animals and a variety of little boxes, papers, wooden craft sticks and fabric. I invited William to help me with my project of creating safe homes for the animals. He grabbed a lion right away and started trying out different sized boxes, choosing one and making a little bed in the corner out of cotton balls and fabric. He watched as I took a tiny brown cow and tried to find a good box to make a home out of. I said out loud: "I wonder what would help a cow feel safe?" William answered right away: "My lion likes a good door so he can let friends in or keep them out!"

The lion's home was getting decorated with beads glued to the top of it, and the cow had a pretty nice green paper yard. As we talked, I learned about how William thought and solved problems and what things he felt were important for someone to feel safe. I learned that surprises weren't good and the lion needed a tiny calendar so he would know what he was going to do each day. The lion's yard got some green grass too, and a big blue strip of paper became a river running between the lion and the cow's houses.

Some things we wondered about included:

- Lions and cows aren't usually friends. Should we help them become friends?

- How do animals, and people, get to know each other? William thought they should tell each other what they like, so we did that and found out that they both liked ice cream.
- What are lions and cows afraid of? The lion was quite afraid of the "bad lions" at lion school.

We realized that the lion and cow couldn't play together because of the river running between their homes. That sparked the creation of the Sparkle Bridge. Created with wooden craft sticks and plenty of purple glitter, it glowed rather magically in its spot over the river. Lion and cow were happy to visit each other's yards and run around chasing each other.

On the way out to reconnect with his dad, William suggested that next time we add more animals and things for them to do to our project.

If we are flexible and interested in following the child's lead, we usually find an early place of connection.

Sometimes a child will spot a puzzle or a game and be intrigued. Following the child's lead feels important to me, so we'll try what they're interested in trying. If it's a puzzle, after we figure it out, I introduce the idea of a puzzle about them that we can create together. I take a piece of paper and have the child help me color one side in (otherwise it will be too confusing to put together). Then I turn it over and cut it into pieces, basing the size and number on the developmental stage the child appears to be in. I invite them to put a picture of what they like in each piece, and then we put them together.

Try the idea out for yourself, using Worksheet #11.

WORKSHEET #11

In each puzzle piece, draw something you like: cut apart and put together!

I remember a small girl trying to make a good picture of a horse because sometimes she got to visit her uncle's farm. She couldn't do it; we couldn't find any collage pictures that worked and so I tried to draw one. I consider making a puzzle together more of a fun activity than actual art therapy so I didn't mind trying to help. But yikes! It turned out that my drawing was ridiculous looking and we started laughing at what a goofy-looking animal I'd made. That laughter completely broke the ice.

The game idea is similar, and perhaps more in-depth. I describe it in *Little windows into art therapy* (2005, p.35) and basically it's creating a blank "game board" on a piece of paper ahead of time. I ask clients to write in events, good and bad, and illustrate the squares. So someone might write "best birthday" on a square, and draw a cake beside the square with instructions to move ahead three spaces. Or a square might say "lost homework" with a sad face and directions to lose a turn. Game pieces can be made out of Play-Doh or they can be small found objects. Using a real dice seems to be the easiest. When we play it, I get to ask a question about what they land on, and when I take my turn they get to ask me a question similar to the square that I landed on. And, yes, I remember losing my homework!

Sometimes, when the session was over and my client and I walked out to the waiting area, I would notice the parent or caregiver giving me that eye contact that seems to ask the question: "Did it go alright?" I would smile and say to both the adult and the child, "I look forward to our next session and getting to know Ginny more."

I consider this first session a success if I've managed to create the beginning of a therapeutic relationship, with at least some eye contact, some interaction, hopefully a smile and maybe even laughter. Going to a therapist can feel like a good experience, even if it's because of something hard.

Chapter 4

ENCOURAGING THE ADULTS IN OUR CLIENTS' LIVES

Often when a parent or caregiver brings a child in for the first time, I hear some version of this: "Our family doesn't really go to therapists, but…" And the "but" was followed by: (1) the school counselor said he needed to see someone; (2) we don't know what to do; or (3) family life has become so hard because of her behavior. I think that in that moment the adult really needs our honest reassurance that many parents bring children to therapy and we don't think that they're "bad parents" for needing to do that. It might be helpful to explore some thoughts about parents and caregivers in Worksheet #12.

WORKSHEET #12

when you think about parents, what comes to mind with these words?

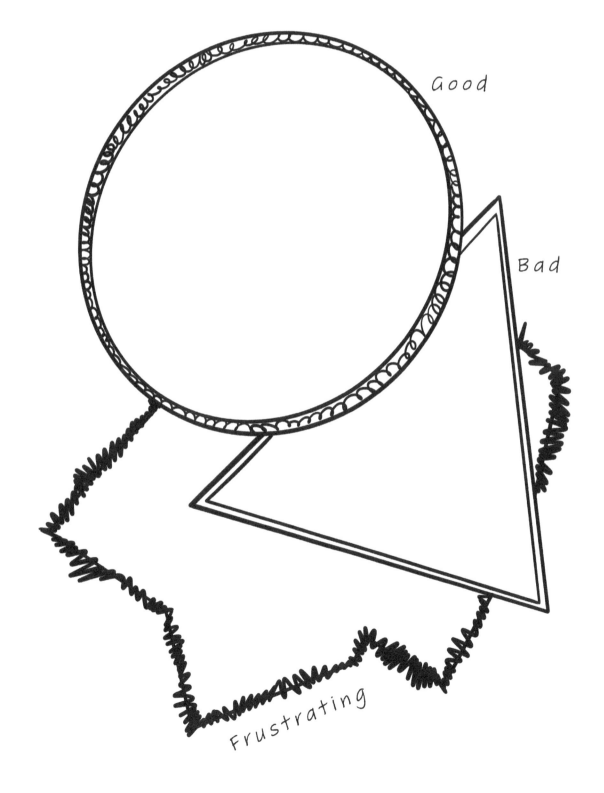

Good

Bad

Frustrating

I've found it useful to name the feelings that come up for me around my own expectations of taking good care of children. And I admit there are some statements I've heard parents say that I have to watch my reactions to. For example, when I ask a parent about their child's strengths, and they say "I don't know" (probably because they're angry or exhausted), I try to remain positive and encourage them to remember.

I don't know many parents, including me, who haven't had moments in parenting when they felt a complete failure. And of course those moments are easier to talk about, and even laugh about, years later when our children have grown up and are living happy lives. My adult children and I can laugh now about how inept I was at successfully communicating anger in a way that didn't make them find it funny.

I approach working with parents from that humble place of trying to parent from a loving heart in the face of a life filled with adult stress. The stress is only made worse by our own expectations of how we "should" parent and how children "should" behave. Mr. Rogers shared these important thoughts:

> If we expect our children to always grow smoothly and steadily and happily, then we're going to worry a lot more than if we are comfortable with the fact that human growth is full of slides backward as well as leaps forward, and is sure to include times of withdrawal, opposition, and anger, just as it encompasses tears as well as laughter. (Rogers, 2006, p.68)

I thought that it would be helpful to talk with a few parents who have taken their children to therapy (not my clients) and share what their child's therapist did that they found useful or unhelpful.

Laura brought her daughter to therapy initially, in order to work on grief issues. Laura herself is a therapist and so she was able to be very clear about what was important to her. She wanted a therapist who didn't pathologize her child and who could "lean into a range of normal" (Laura, personal communication, March 24, 2021)—a therapist who didn't give the message that Laura or her child was bad. The therapist that she found included her in the therapy plans, sharing what was happening with a sense of open communication. The therapist established roles and expectations and a way of working at the onset of therapy, and would begin sessions with both Laura and her daughter present, and then would bring Laura back in again at the end of the session.

Laura felt that it was important for her daughter to choose who brought up topics in therapy, which definitely gave her daughter some power over her own therapeutic work.

Because Laura is a therapist she may have been more comfortable shopping around for a therapist than many parents are. She met a few therapists whom she definitely wasn't comfortable with, and here are some of the issues that she shared with me:

- A therapist quickly made it clear that she knew how to "solve the problem." The writing pair Sommers-Flanagan make it clear that: "the professional needs to hold a collaborative attitude that honors the parents' knowledge and experience" (Sommers-Flanagan & Sommers-Flanagan, 2011, p.11). They also discussed a kind of radical acceptance that involves "letting go of the immediate need to teach parents a new and better way" (Sommers-Flanagan & Sommers-Flanagan, 2011, p.10).
- One therapist was overly business-like, asking for insurance information before trying to understand the situation.
- One became overly emotional when hearing why they were seeking therapy. It isn't the client's job to comfort the therapist.
- Three therapists didn't ask questions about Laura's husband. (I find it astonishing that assumptions were made about a dad's lack of participation, when, in fact, it was a scheduling difficulty.)
- Some therapists didn't show any interest in the family or how life felt at home. "I find it helpful to think of the family as a big tent. Some tents are protective and can withstand the worst gales and weather. Other tents get torn up and collapse in a strong wind. Think about what kind of tent each child lives under and how you might be able to patch or reinforce its weaknesses" (Shannon, 2013, pp.93–94). Laura's family was clearly a strong tent, and she clearly wanted a therapist who would value the family's beliefs and culture and who would treat her daughter with respect and dignity. Laura was tuned in to any subtle ways that a therapist might imply parental blame or disrespect. As mental health practitioners are now examining how we can decolonize mental health, I deeply believe that not only should we be interested in a family's cultural beliefs, but that it's time to look at our client's mental health issues in the context of the place or area in which they live. We need to consider factors like safety, transportation, accessibility to services, food accessibility and affordable housing. This kind of assessment of the environment can say much about what children and parents struggle with—issues that impact the stress of daily life.

I think that the therapist who worked with Laura's daughter was fortunate in knowing that Laura understood the therapeutic process. Not everyone, though, who brings a child to therapy has experienced therapy themselves.

I spoke with Cynthia, who brought her son to therapy when he was around nine, because she and her husband were separating. Cynthia's son was furious and took his anger out at both homes, but especially with his mom. Cynthia wasn't sure about what to expect from therapy or how the process might work for her son. "Educating parents about the therapy process is essential. Unless parents understand and know what I am doing, they can easily sabotage the work. Parent education becomes a vital part of the therapy process and most parents are grateful for it" (Oaklander, 2007, p.48).

Cynthia's son saw several different therapists and made progress in his ability to communicate with each parent, which, over time, decreased his angry outbursts. Cynthia noted that one family services agency had numerous offices for therapists and, as they walked by them, they never saw a kid-friendly office. Every office was clearly furnished with adults in mind. One therapist that her son saw at least had small items to fidget with and hold, but another one didn't have anything and the expectation was that a child client would be able to sit and talk.

Cynthia commented that her son never saw a therapist of his own race, and that didn't seem to be an obstacle in therapy. He did seem more open with a male therapist. Cynthia was invited into the session with this particular therapist every other session, and she found that very helpful. I asked her why therapy had ended and she said that during the pandemic only phone sessions could be arranged with the agency's therapists and no video sessions were offered. Her son wasn't as interested and engaged during phone sessions and therapy seemed much less effective. At least it would seem that the prior in-person therapy will make it more likely her son would consider returning to therapy if life became more difficult for him (Cynthia, personal communication, May 2, 2021).

Another parent, Samantha, and her husband, sought therapy for their daughter after a move across town triggered an extremely difficult time for her daughter. Her daughter wouldn't open up to them, was sad and angry, disobeying rules and then ran away from home. When they saw the therapist, his calm, warm presence was reassuring to Samantha and her husband and seemed to help their daughter connect with him. She met with him every week for about three years, and said that her daughter liked him and never argued about going to therapy.

Samantha and her husband only met with him three or four times, and always felt that he genuinely cared. He upheld the confidentiality and he never told them what their daughter said in therapy and so her daughter trusted that she could say whatever she needed to, to him. He recognized their daughter's level of depression after a few initial sessions and referred the family to a psychiatrist for additional support. Samantha said, about the therapist, "I believe he saved her life. We couldn't reach her" (Samantha, personal communication, May 16, 2021).

Samantha mentioned that it was a very emotional experience for the family when therapy was finished and it was time to say goodbye to him.

There are certainly rather predictable times in family life when it's good to seek out a therapist for a struggling child. For Samantha's family it began with a move across town. For many families, it is the timeframe before, during and after a divorce or break-up.

Feelings brought by the parent and the child to that first therapy session can be quite raw and close to the surface. Clarity of one's role as a therapist is imperative. Will you be focusing only on the child, or will you provide psychoeducation and support to one or both parents? Mediation between parents is something very different from psychoeducation and support, and referrals could be given if that's what the parents expect.

"Most divorcing and recently divorced parents are in a great deal of distress and need comfort, support, and information" (Sommers-Flanagan & Sommers-Flanagan, 2011, p.199). Rick and his husband Thomas sought therapy for their six-year-old son because of his difficult behaviors during their separation and their divorce. During the first session, both parents were present. Rick didn't believe that it started off well and spoke about the therapist seeming eager to tell them how to manage his behavior before she had really gotten to know them (Rick, personal communication, April 17, 2021). The Sommers-Flanagans would both agree: "premature educational interventions can carry an inherently judgmental message" (Sommers-Flanagan & Sommers-Flanagan, 2011, p.13).

Spending time conveying respect and empathy will definitely create a therapeutic container for offering helpful ideas further down the road. I try to remember that the child client knows themselves, and the parent or guardian knows the child in the context of their family, home, neighborhood and culture, in a way that I absolutely will never know.

When I feel like I have a sense of the child, and the parent, I do like to try and encourage them in some activities to remind them that they can enjoy each other's company. I like to offer some homework that promotes casual, pleasant interactions. We want adults to show that they are willing to make some special time with their child each week; that they *enjoy* their child and *want* to spend time with them. I acknowledge the difficulty that can present for busy, working parents, but positive attention can often decrease the need for children to seek attention in some negative way.

Some ideas of activities include:

- The goofiest pancake contest with all members of the family who can be present. The adult makes strangely shaped pancakes (I don't have to try to do that!), and people can decorate with anything available, fruit, raisins, syrup, chocolate chips, nut spreads, etc.

- Give the child and parent a copy of Worksheet #13, the aquarium. As homework, have them ask each family member to draw what they would be in the family aquarium. Who knows what will be in there—a shark, a fast little fish, a mermaid, a treasure chest or a fish that cleans up the aquarium? If the child brings it back the next week, it's a fun way to get to know who's in the family.
- A "What can we find?" walk. The adult(s) and child take a walk together and collect leaves, interesting scraps and tiny rocks to make a picture with. They can make the picture at home or the child can bring in the stuff to the next session.
- Be a nice neighbor. The child and an adult choose a neighbor to do something nice for, bring treats to or make a card for.
- Make a tent. We know that kids love to take a blanket and drape it over something and hide away in it. What if the adult helps make it, and then reads a book to the child inside the tent?
- Movie night, and it's the child's choice of movie and snacks, and the adult watches the whole movie with the child. This feels different from "putting a movie on" for a child and then leaving the room or doing something else.
- Interview a parent or grandparent. Help the child think of a few questions they would like to know from an adult in their family. Write them down for the child and, if the child can write, they can write the answer themselves when they talk to the adult. Otherwise, the adult can write down the answers or the story. When the child comes to the next session you can ask them what they found out.

WORKSHEET #13

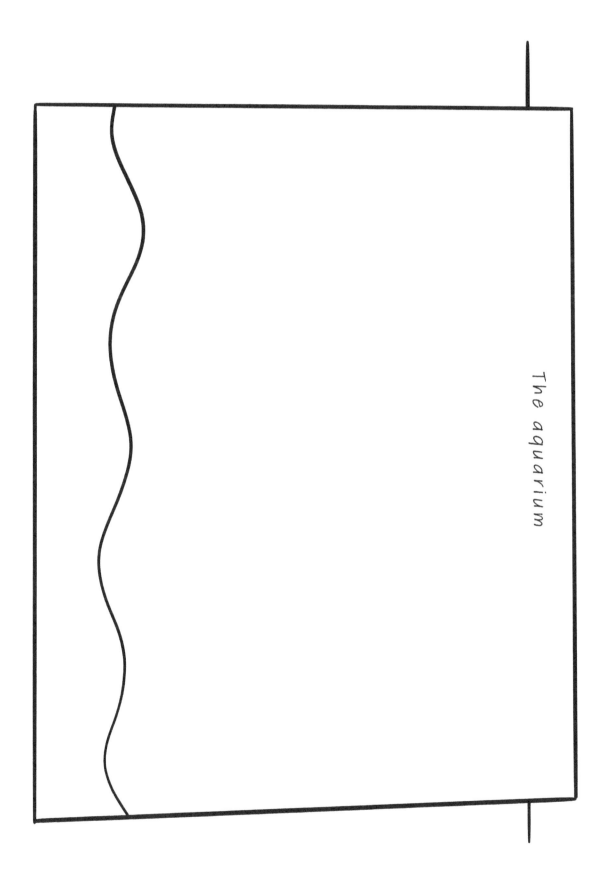

The aquarium

Chapter 5

WHEN THE ISSUE IS ANGER

Noah smiled and said hello when his dad brought him to our first session. He looked like any eight year old at the end of a school day, a little tired and rumpled. He didn't fit the description that his dad gave me on the phone, which seemed to suggest a spinning tornado that kicked things. He played Lego while his dad did the initial paperwork and talked with me about why it was time for therapy. Noah didn't look up, but focused intently on what he was building when his dad described some recent explosions.

When his dad left, Noah and I worked together on some buildings and a spaceship while I explained who I was and what we might do together when he saw me. We really didn't talk about anger; I think I said something like, "Your mom and dad think you might be kind of upset about something. What do you think?" He looked up and said, "Nope, I'm fine."

It took a solid relationship and a bunny puppet provoking a tiger puppet for me to hear some anger. We did eventually get to that subject after we had a trusting relationship built. He liked puppets so one day I invited him to show me, with a puppet, how he would know if his sister was happy. He picked a bright bird puppet and spun it around and sang with a high-pitched voice, "La, la, la, I'm so happy, Danny talked to me today!" It was impossible for us not to laugh at this clever depiction of his happy older sister.

I like to explore with young clients how members of their family show emotions. I try and start with an easy one, like happy, and eventually get to sad, scared and angry. Families have some amazing spoken and unspoken rules about emotions, especially anger. I've had clients who couldn't ever show anger and who spent a lot of time in their rooms if they "talked back" or yelled at a parent. Of course therapists are curious about how parents show anger, if a child is exploding at home. I'm also curious if the explosions are happening at school or with friends or in other social experiences. What seems to be going on when they *don't* happen? What's been going on that might make a person sad or worried in the family?

When Noah and I got to looking at "sad" he picked a dinosaur puppet and put it under a blanket. We figured out together that it seemed better to him to hide "sad," because he believed it was pretty contagious—if he was sad then everyone else might get sad too. The large size of the dinosaur also seemed significant. Was "sad" pretty huge for him? All other members of the family were portrayed as quiet when sad.

I would never pretend that therapy went in a straight line. A few weeks in, his parents wondered what we were doing, since the temper explosions weren't settling down.

We kept playing and talking—none of the puppets representing family members showed much anger, except when the bright bird sister yelled at him to stay out of her room. Noah just grinned at that little moment of drama. He chose a tiger puppet. I took the bunny puppet and hopped over to the tiger: "Hi tiger, hope you aren't looking for a bunny!"

Tiger laughed, we kidded around about a bunny and a tiger having a conversation, and then the bunny blurted out, "So how would I know if you were angry?"

Tiger let out a roar, and then a bigger one. Bunny hopped around saying "Wow!", and tiger let out a huge roar, and I saw a tiny tear in his eye.

I said, in my therapist voice, not bunny voice, "What are you feeling right now?" And Noah finally said that he was so mad and sad that his Grandpa had died and no one else seemed to care. Grandpa had died about six months ago but no one mentioned it when I asked about family and family life. People often don't think to mention things that they've tried to put in the past or tried very hard to not think about.

We had some good conversations with Dad first, since Grandpa was his father. Mr. Rogers understood the importance of parents sharing and modeling their emotions:

I remember after my grandfather's death, seeing Dad in the hall with tears streaming down his face. I don't think I had ever seen him cry before. I'm glad I did see him. It helped me know that it was okay for men to cry. Many years later, when my father himself died, I cried; and way down deep I knew he would have said it was all right. (Rogers, 2003, p.29)

Anger can be quite skillfully used to cover up all kinds of feelings. And sometimes we build relationships with kids who do come in angry and their families hold anger as something that can get loud and big and then go away. I had some young clients who needed to figure out how to have a few seconds' pause at school to keep their anger from getting loud and big. And sometimes during the first few sessions, some of my clients haven't enjoyed my curiosity about their anger and my thoughts about calming. I've seen small humans glare at me and heard them say: "I know how to breathe!" A sense of humor in that moment really helps. It's good to think about how you react to angry humans, big or small. Try Worksheets #14 and #15 as you think about this.

WORKSHEET #14

How did your family members express anger?

_____

_____

_____

_____

_____

_____

_____

How did you express anger as a child?

_____

_____

_____

_____

_____

_____

_____

WORKSHEET #15

How comfortable are you with your own anger now?

How comfortable are you with someone else's anger?

I know how important it is to help kids find a tiny pause before acting impulsively in anger. "Emotional competence is the ability to be aware of feelings but also take account of what you think before you decide on a course of action" (Hooper, 2012, p.78).

And sometimes it needs to be realized that the expression of that anger is more of a systemic problem and really is a family therapy issue.

Alongside the expression of anger is the repair that may be needed, and it's a wonderful parenting moment when an adult can apologize for words said in anger.

Chapter 6

MY TUMMY HURTS

One of my sisters had quite a few tummy aches before school when she was little. Back then I don't think adults really believed her. Now we have a clearer understanding of somatic body–brain connections, and we understand that anxiety can be the cause of stomach problems, headaches, digestive issues and all of the many symptoms associated with panic attacks, like shortness of breath, rapid heartbeats, sweating, feeling unreal, feeling like you're not in your body or that a part of your body isn't "normal," dizziness, wanting to get out of wherever you are and the feeling that you're going to die. If a child hears the well-meaning but negative message that "It's nothing," "You're okay," "Just quit it and go do something," the child may feel truly crazy and want to isolate. Building a relationship with a child who has anxiety takes an extra dose of calm on the part of the therapist. A presence of calm combined with genuinely welcoming and believing the child's experience will lead to a trusting relationship. Use Worksheet #16 to name your childhood worries. What kind of worries did you have growing up? Who could you tell?

WORKSHEET #16

What did you worry about as a child?

Hang on to any of those?

The reasons behind all this worry vary from child to child. Some kids worry about everything. Some kids worry about one specific thing. Some kids subtly, or not so subtly, learn to worry about things from their parents. Some kids live in anxious family systems where everyone kind of vibrates with whatever is in the atmosphere. "There are a variety of presentations; the important thing here is to look at how much stress and anxiety kids are under and how well they are able to relax and unwind. Also, look at a child's apprehensiveness, insomnia, fears, worry, tension, separation issues, controlling style, and a variety of somatic issues like headaches and migraines" (Shannon, 2013, p.113). I think it can often be helpful for the parent or caregiver to tell you what kind of things they worry about or share out loud at home. You can ask them to fill Worksheet #17 out, or you can fill it out together.

WORKSHEET #17

Parents and caregivers, kids pick up on so much! What kinds of things do you worry about?

_____

_____

_____

_____

_____

_____

_____

_____

_____

_____

_____

thank you

When a bad thing happens within a family or neighborhood, kids can believe that the door to all bad things has opened up and they're watching and waiting for someone to get sick or go away or die, or not love them anymore. While adults are aware that any bad thoughts they have about someone are just thoughts, they know that they can't magically harm any person who they're mad at, "Some children feel anxious because they imagine themselves doing something bad, hurting themselves or someone else" (O'Neill, 2019, p.29).

We want to take any concrete thoughts and plans to hurt self or others seriously, of course. And honestly, I saw a number of young clients who shared that they thought such mad things about someone that now they worried constantly that the person would be hurt somehow or even die.

What mysteries to explore, what's happening in life that makes someone have such big worries? If a child's worries have been dismissed in any way by another adult, the child may believe that I'm going to dismiss their fears too. They often would whisper or cry when they told me, and that took some relationship-building time to happen. Some worries seem especially hard for adults and children to share. Think for a moment about worries that you don't easily open up about, and use Worksheet #18 to note them.

WORKSHEET #18

what worries are hard for you to share?

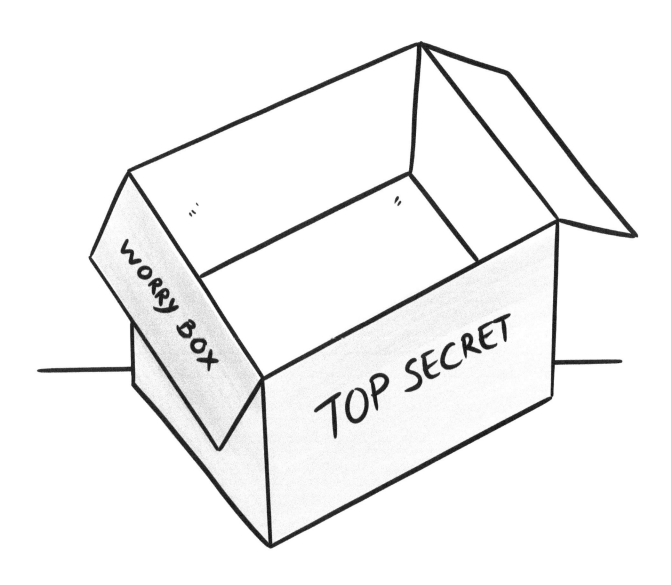

We know that as adults we often have a hard time concentrating when we're anxious. An anxious child at school can have a terribly difficult time with focus. Sometimes those kids are thought to be daydreaming or inattentive and are brought to therapy. I remember a young child who appeared to "drift away" during the entire time her class was studying fractions because she was worried about something happening at home and how awful it might be when she got there. Drifting away happened most easily during fraction time because she wasn't that interested in the subject in the first place.

I spoke with Magdalena, who was a school counselor for many years. She talked about an issue related to the school day that I had experienced as a parent but hadn't looked at as a mental health professional: "The beginning of the school day is hard, going from one environment to another. Families have all kinds of struggles in the morning, getting up, getting ready, eating. Parents have varying abilities to organize that" (Magdalena, personal communication, August 10, 2021). I remember that whirlwind pace of trying to pack lunches, offer some kind of breakfast, remind about putting homework in backpacks, find the missing shoe, veto outfits and somehow express, "Have a great day!", while trying to get myself ready for work. I wonder, now, how flustered and wound up my children were before they even stepped into the classroom. Magdalena also talked about the need many students have to code switch. The more different the home environment is from the classroom, the more complicated that can be. Consider things like literally different languages, different sounds and noise levels, different ways of relating to other humans, especially authority figures, and the myriad different life experiences. Kids can experience such anxiety with transitions and some are better at adapting than others—they seem to have an understanding of how to scan the environment and then adapt to the system in which they find themselves. Therapists can utilize creative skills in helping children tell the story that they aren't consciously aware of having a role in. Play, art and pretend can all open the door to all that happens before a school day begins.

I especially appreciated Magdalena's statement that as a therapist we can't assume that we're safe for somebody. I know that I unconsciously held that belief at times, seeing the world through the lens of my experience and whom I would have found safe as a child.

In her work in a school setting, Magdalena spoke about trying to match the pace of the child. If the child presented as quiet and slow, she would also be quiet and slow. A faster, more animated child might need to start the session by walking, going outside or ripping paper up.

She also had some important thoughts on working with parents and spoke about not taking on the needs of the parents. While maintaining good boundaries with parents, she also understood that parenting is hard. She cautions that therapists should "check their biases" about what families are "supposed" to look like.

As we build relationships with our young, anxious clients, I think it's especially important to offer appropriate psychoeducation when the issue appears to be anxiety, normalizing what reactions our bodies have, what happens when we sense danger and how hard our bodies work to keep us safe. Can we learn to appreciate our brain, and then talk about what reactions we might be able to choose to let go of? Sometimes I would share that I had some fast fear happen when I heard angry voices, and I wanted to run and hide. Good job, brain, for offering a solution, but I needed to come up with some other ways of soothing and calming that let me stay in the home, classroom or workplace. "The single best stress management tool is focused counseling examining stress triggers and exploring resources and coping tools" (Shannon, 2013, p.109). Shannon continues by offering ideas such as yoga, meditation, exercise, time in nature, sunshine, time with animals and long walks.

An initial idea that I might use in the beginning of a relationship with an anxious child might be to create a "magic carpet." I would offer a piece of hemmed muslin, long enough for a child to sit on or even lie down on if they wanted to. The child could decorate it with fabric crayons in any way that they wanted, and use it at home as a calming space, imagining being surrounded by anything that helped them feel peaceful. For kids who moved between households this portable calm space seemed especially appreciated.

Another good project can be a tiny treasure bag. I would make or buy a tiny fabric bag and a young client could choose and place something in it that felt helpful when a sudden moment of anxiety came—maybe a small pebble or seashell, a marble or a bead and a sprig of lavender.

And sometimes what was needed was some kind of movement. Six-year-old Jeff and I created and decorated "shakers," which were sealed containers with beans inside, and he used them when he needed to shake anxiety away before trying a new experience with his family. The noise was as important as the jumping around that accompanied it. Sometimes in session we would do some shaking before talking about something hard.

A lingering benefit from the pandemic seems to be adults' heightened awareness of the impact of anxiety upon their own psyches. It is to be hoped that we all learned a few practices or techniques to soothe our own anxiety. Parents can share their own experiences and how they quiet themselves or center themselves when feeling anxious. Of course, what works for a 35 year old might not have the same effect on a child. Listening to soothing piano music might not be as helpful as blowing bubbles.

I appreciate these words about children and anxiety:

The lives that children lead now are more stressful and demanding than in previous generations. Children are bombarded with expectations from many sources: home and school, their peer group and what they see in the media. These expectations are not always aligned with each other and conflicting expectations can lead to confusion. The uncertainty about direction and boundaries create the potential for stress, anxiety and unhappiness. (Hooper, 2012, p.26)

Chapter 7

WHERE DO I BELONG?

The world of adults and their relationships can swirl like an ever-changing river or be a still, quiet pond. Relationships can ebb and flow like the ocean's tide, or rush quickly through twists and turns like a fast-moving stream. In New Mexico it's often said "stay out of the arroyos when it rains"—water comes gushing quickly through the dry landscape. Children, in the flow of their parents' relationship, are along for the ride, sometimes clutching at their floating inner-tubes, having no control over the direction or speed of the water. It could be useful to use Worksheet #19 at this point.

WORKSHEET #19

when you were a child, what was your
experience of your parents' relationship?

_____

_____

_____

_____

_____

_____

_____

Any other significant adults in your
childhood?

_____

_____

_____

_____

_____

I have empathy for the adults who are trying to make healthy decisions for their own lives while nurturing their children. I also have much empathy for children who have their sense of hope and family shaken up by separation, divorce and all the stages of adults trying to be in relationships. "This does not mean that no child of divorce will find happiness or good mental health; it just means it has become harder and will require more work and attention" (Shannon, 2013, p.48).

A solution that usually is grappled with when parents separate is how to share the kids and share parenting responsibilities. This can leave kids in that place of having multiple homes with perhaps even new adults or children present.

When a child is brought to us because of parental separation, we need to be completely open to the child's various responsibilities, fears, anger and sadness. I treat the first session with these children exactly like any first session.

An early issue is figuring out how to focus completely on what the child needs in that moment—playing, making art, maybe not talking a lot.

Early in our sessions I would ask to see "Who is in your world?", inviting the child to show me anyone they consider family, in the sandtray, with toys, with stuffed animals or with art. That helps me try to get an understanding of who's who in the child's lived experience. I invite you to do a similar exercise using Worksheet #20 in order to be in touch with your feelings about who was in your world as a child.

WORKSHEET #20

Kids try and make sense out of who is in their world. Remember your world of people as a kid. How did you organize them?

(You can add more circles)

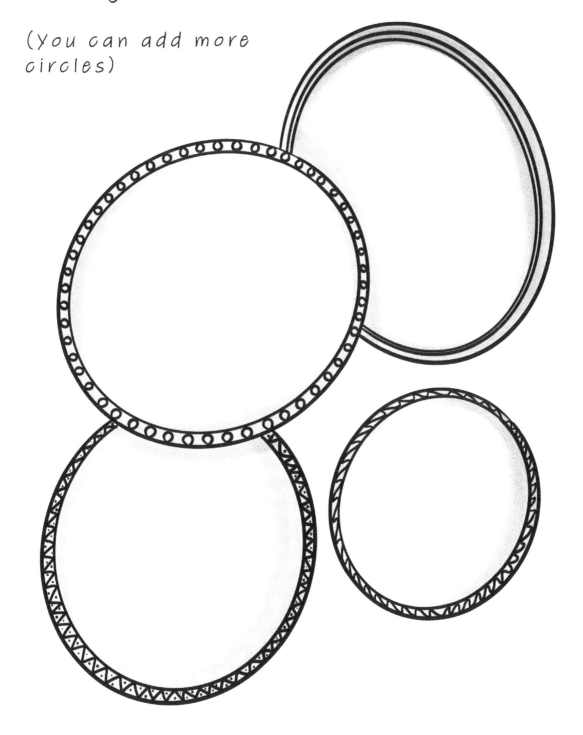

Children will often figure out how to separate the groups of people and pets visually. Figurines or toys are often grouped according to the separation. When everyone in the child's world is scattered more randomly, I might ask the child to show me who lives with whom, or which Grandpa goes with which parent. The big struggle is often about where children place themselves. The visual problem is quite representative of the very real human problem. Children often leave themselves out of the scene, quite literally not knowing where they belong.

Creating therapeutic relationships with children in this situation requires special attention to helping them trust your confidentiality. If they do need to say, someday, that they're unhappy with a parent, stepparent or grandparent, they need to know that you can hold that information.

I found that while parents are deeply concerned about their child's well-being, the back and forth of where and when the child moves between them is often determined by work schedules and activities of the parents. We need to be very clear about who our client is. If we are the child's therapist, it is to be hoped that someone else is helping the parents explore the complicated issues of co-parenting. If parents tended to hold different parenting responsibilities while together, those responsibilities may need to be shared differently now that they're apart. Knowing whom to go to for what is one of the many issues that surface for our young clients.

The movement from home to home is an area of struggle for many children. We can be compassionate listeners to statements like: "I can't sleep at Dad's apartment," "I don't like sharing a room with Mom's boyfriend's son" and "I don't like the food at that house," etc. For very young children, just the sadness of missing a parent when with the other parent can be painful. With parents' help, I liked to create little travel kits that could go back and forth, even if it was just down the street: a happy picture of the parent, maybe a happy note from the parent and a piece of fabric with the parent's fragrance or cologne. This seemed to empower the child to have a tool to use when missing someone.

With older children, I often experienced a very firm commitment, on their part, to being "fine." It felt important to stay with the getting-to-know-you phase for a longer while because eventually we might get to explore the core parts of my young client that hadn't changed while everything around them felt like it had changed.

I don't think it's our job to convince children that they're not fine. Maybe our exploration of emotions will help normalize that there are shades of fine—we can be ourselves and feel kind of sad. If being fine is part of trying to take care of a parent's feelings, being able to not be completely fine with a therapist can be a relief.

A complicated variety of not totally fine can be guilt. Children often believe that they have somehow caused the situation between their parents and carry around the belief that they are secretly responsible as if they are carrying a heavy stone that can't be put down.

In a perfect world, parents and grandparents would kindly welcome new caring adults into their child's world, and no one would ever say unpleasant things about the other parent. "It can be difficult for divorcing parents to talk with their children without blaming the other parent. This can be either blatant or subtle" (Sommers-Flanagan & Sommers-Flanagan, 2011, p.200). And as someone who has divorced a spouse, this was easier said than done. I didn't ask but I did hear some ridiculous, hurtful statements made about me. And I know that my face and tone of voice told my children what I thought about their dad feeding them pizza again. Co-parenting after a separation requires an inner commitment concerning things said and unsaid that wavers in the face of strong emotions at times. And children hear their adults and feel confused. "Children always try to make sense of what goes on in their lives, and feel frustrated and confused most of the time" (Oaklander, 2007, p.38). Therapists are trying to develop relationships with their young clients during what may seem like, to the child, the worst time ever in their lives. They've heard and observed such hard things from the adults they love. When writing about children's well-being, child psychologist Scott Shannon stated: "if the parents have divorced or if the marriage is strained, everything is much more complicated, both for the child and for the practitioner" (Shannon, 2013, p.45).

I found that having a very predictable routine for therapy sessions for children whose family life is turned upside down is particularly important. They need to know that they can trust the sameness; no surprises.

Chapter 8

MOVING INTO DEEPER WORK

I was so pleased when child psychologists April and Carlos agreed to talk with me. Their warmth and open communication made it clear why they both are wonderfully suited to work with children. I was interested in how they moved into deeper work, or the "real issues" with children.

Carlos began by speaking about the need to recognize that children are not little adults and that looking at their world through a developmental lens was important. Children understand their experiences in a developmentally concrete way. Therapy with adolescents can look more like adult therapy as they can understand the use of abstract thought (Carlos, personal communication, November 18, 2021).

As Carlos continued, he emphasized the important relationship building that happens by following the child's lead, while remembering that children are physical and speak using non-verbal communication that happens in play and symbolic representation.

"Relational healing occurs in many ways because each child and helping professional constitute a unique and dynamic relationship. However, it is most often demonstrated to young clients by the therapist's ability to be flexible, playful, and creative in responding to what children bring to treatment" (Malchiodi & Crenshaw, 2017, p.14).

He definitely found getting down on the floor, being with them, important. Carlos mentioned Winnicott's work and I went back to a text I remembered from grad. school: "It is good to remember always that playing is itself a therapy. To arrange for children to play is itself a psychotherapy that has immediate and universal application, and it includes the establishment of a positive social attitude towards playing" (Winnicott, 1971, p.50).

April spoke up and shared the idea that the work starts before one is in the room with the child. She agreed with Carlos that a solid understanding of the age range one works with was vital: "What is typical, what are the developmental milestones? What is typical in terms of emotional, physical and cognitive development" (April, personal communication, November 18, 2021).

Both were thoughtful about what materials were placed out. Having an abundance of options lets therapists see how the child moves between choices. And initially the presence of the parent in the room lets the therapist witness how the child moves between the safe base of the parent and the therapist. During this foundational phase of the relationship, as the therapist follows the child's lead, they can observe what the child gravitates toward, watching, listening and mirroring. The therapist might hold three or four hypotheses at once, trying things out and checking the responses. Shannon, in *Mental health for the whole child*, offered these thoughts:

> holistic assessment emphasizes the deeper impressions and intuitions that we all have. The goal is not to form impressions quickly, but to allow impression to form, to "take it all in," as it were. Later this will empower the intuitive process as you work with someone. The more quiet and accepting you can be, the better this information can be collected. (Shannon, 2013, p.178)

Playing on the floor, and the ability to engage in play, seemed important and they made the suggestion that a therapist try out their own office by shutting the door and playing! I think that's a brilliant idea, and I encourage you to try it and reflect on your own experience with Worksheet #21.

WORKSHEET #21

what was it like to play in your office?

what was fun?

what was missing?

what did you see
from the floor?

They agreed that kids will often tell us non-verbally if we're pushing too hard when getting at the main issue. Children will move away and change toys or their play abruptly. Carlos mentioned that it might take the relationship a month or more of sessions before the child is ready to do the work concerning the issue they were brought into therapy for.

I appreciated that they both believe in limit setting and establishing boundaries before attempting to do deeper work. Children will test to see what the limits are, find out what the rules are. Knowing what one's rules are as a therapist before being in the room with a child seems important (April & Carlos, personal communication, November 18, 2021). The careful opening and establishing of relationships helps provide the containment for what needs to surface.

In their commitments to follow the child's lead, it seems that through careful observation they understand when to pause, and how to respect a child's hesitancy around certain issues. Carlos suggested sitting outside, getting out of the office. He spoke about some therapy rituals that could be helpful sometimes, like sharing a snack together and talking while enjoying that treat. (I remember that often parents would bring children in right after school or sports practice and they were hungry. With parental permission and knowledge of what kids couldn't have, a snack can be a kind way to connect.) April said that she often kept a basket of things for kids to fidget with near where they sat.

In art therapy, we often find that an image might show up in a surprisingly unprepared for, unanticipated, fast way. It sometimes felt to me as though the image that showed up was just bursting out of someone's psyche, before the client was really ready to explore that particular issue being named by the image. This happens with children too, and we might know that they feel they're "in too deep" by observing them literally getting away from the image, dropping it on the floor, throwing it in the garbage or scribbling over it. I would save the image from destruction when appropriate (sometimes the destruction was a very vital part of the art process) and say that I would keep it safe for them in case they wanted to look at it again someday. And children would remember that, and ask weeks later if I could bring it out for them. I like to consider that art is often predictive of where the therapy path needs to go.

At the end of a session that had moved into some uncomfortable depth, I found it important to talk about that a little and say that next week my client could pick a game or an art media choice to start with, letting them know that I didn't expect to go right back to the uncomfortable topic again. And sometimes the child would think about it during the week and come in wanting to talk some more about it. More often, we would wade slowly back to that depth, titrating between easy and uncomfortable.

On occasion, I would invite the parent or caregiver in the room, so I could share that their child had done some important work today, and we would talk together about how they might make the rest of the child's day as easy and stress-free as possible.

Chapter 9

CONNECTING WITH TWEENS

When my youngest granddaughter was about one year old, we all became aware of her rather independent personality. She knew what she wanted to do, and tried to do it. We smiled and nodded and someone said "Just wait until she's a teenager, watch out!" Adults often forget that there's a definite pre-adolescent stage that also requires parents' acceptance and guidance—the tween years. Of course it would be helpful to reconnect with your own memories of those years by completing Worksheet #22.

WORKSHEET #22

what did you see in the mirror

when you were a tween?

I hope that we all find some compassion for whoever that tween was during those years. Our own understanding, empathy and perhaps even forgiveness toward our own self during that time can be so useful when we work with our young clients.

Many of the same issues that might prompt parents or caregivers to bring a child to therapy are similar to why they might bring a tween to therapy. Plus some that might surface a little in childhood but become more intense between the ages of about 9 and 12.

When I think about creating a therapeutic relationship with a tween, the words "watchful observation" come to mind. We aren't greeting and getting to know a child or a teenager, we're trying to know someone who also is trying to know who they are.

Tweens may be especially sensitive to hearing what parents are saying about them during an initial session. Parents may talk about them or to them, the way they would a child, because in many respects their child is still quite childlike. This can make the intake session rather stormy. I try to make zero assumptions about what a tween might gravitate toward in my office. When May's mom left the room I noticed that May kept looking at a shelf with self-hardening clay on it. I didn't ask her if she wanted to play with it; instead I said "I've always loved that stuff," and she said that she used to, and I asked her if she remembered what she used to make. We each took some in different colors and she flattened hers and then rolled the clay into a lovely rose. As we talked she kept squishing it and reforming things with it and so did I. We had something to do together without naming it as something her child-self enjoyed. She did decide to keep her creations and let them harden.

The ability to fluidly engage with a tween requires a way of listening that usually meant I felt the need to pause and reflect before speaking. The pause gave me a moment to understand the underlying need. Was there a child's need for safety or nurturing evident or was there a yearning for respect and independence? I wanted to show my utmost respect for the developing adolescent, while still being able to access my own sense of fun and play. Again, the ability of a therapist to laugh and be playful seems like a requirement if one is seeing children or tweens.

A useful exploration for many clients is often the difference between how they experience themselves on the inside and how they present themselves to the world on the outside. This kind of exploration translates well into an art or writing activity. Boxes or masks lend themselves to an "inside/outside" exploration, especially if one emphasizes that the inside of the mask doesn't have to be shared; neither does the box have to be opened.

Tweens move at their own pace between who's most present on the inside and outside. May would often come in with her adolescent presence visible, and sometimes pretty angry at the world of authority figures. And frequently she could relax and share a fear or sadness that she'd felt the need to try and hide. She seemed to choose clothing that camouflaged her body and its beginning changes. Tweens' bodies, brains and emotional worlds can be swirling rapidly, creating a kaleidoscope of identity issues. This can make the tween experience feel like an endless transition.

Some of the identity issues were part of who they were as very tiny children. As they grow and move toward adolescence these issues cry out for adult compassion and support. "However, parents and professionals alike may feel uncertain how to support, discuss, or raise the issue of healthy sexual development, and this becomes more challenging when children and adolescents have identities falling outside of what is considered 'heteronormative' or 'gender binary'" (Smelser, 2021, p.91). Our tween clients may have important reasons to be particularly anxious about gender and sexuality questions: "85% of LGBTQ youth rate their stress as higher than 5 on a 1–5 scale" (Smelser, 2021, p.91).

Before we consider how to welcome our young vulnerable clients with their questions about gender and sexuality, therapists need to find their inner stillness where they can explore their beliefs and biases. Please use Worksheet #23 to bring yours to your awareness.

WORKSHEET #23

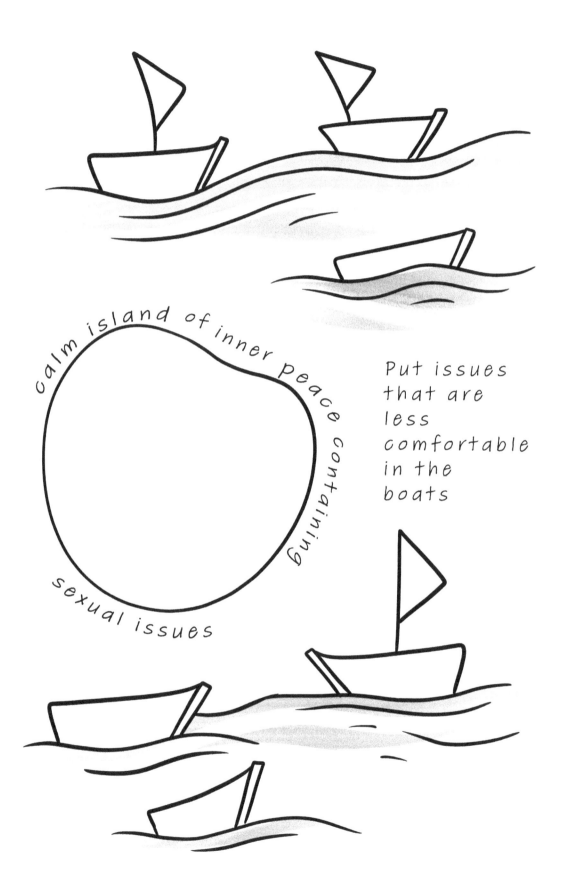

calm island of inner peace containing sexual issues

Put issues that are less comfortable in the boats

Learning and growing as adults is healthy and we can be gentle with ourselves for not knowing what we didn't know, if we are intentional about researching, learning and being open to new understandings.

Humans don't choose the socioeconomic circumstances they are born into, or their race, culture, health, physical and cognitive abilities. Humans also don't choose gender identity; this kind of knowing who one is grows in awareness and development or can be quite clear from early on.

While curiosity about bodies and genitalia may happen early in childhood, our very young clients and often our tween clients are quite gender expansive, trying to live with an openness about who they are or who they may become. Smelser wrote about the time of middle childhood, ages 9 to 11, when sexual and affectional feelings and orientation are being explored and identified. Sexual preference is different from gender identity.

I believe that a therapeutic relationship can offer the safety and space for any issues that a child or tween brings to their play, art, talking and writing. And tweens aren't always brought to therapy to intentionally explore these issues. These identity or sexual issues may organically surface if our offices, toys, games, etc. are affirming in all possible ways. Smelser includes an important list of best practices for play therapists who work with LGBTQ youth and families in the book *Cultural issues in play therapy* (2021, pp.98–102).

My young client May was most interested in how she was perceived by adults in her interactions at home and school. She wanted to have a voice in her rules and the areas of her identity that held her expanding interests. She didn't want to play the flute anymore. She wanted to learn rock climbing. She wanted to have unchaperoned time with her friends. Some of this growth brought some unexpected sadness. She decided to give her dolls to her younger sister and was teary the day she told me about it. It was as though this giving up of something she loved was her own personally created rite of passage. "Experiencing loss is an essential part of ordinary growth and development. It can often be the spur to change and psychological maturity" (Graham & Midgley, 2020, p.40). Therapists are in a good spot to explore and sometimes question those things that tweens believe must be "given up."

Parents and caregivers may also bring their own confusion to their relationships with tweens. I know a mom who was hurt when her daughter announced that she didn't need their bedtime ritual anymore, stating that it was "for kids." As Mom kind of withdrew behind an emotional wall, her daughter reacted to this perceived disinterest by getting attention in more negative ways, complaining about almost everything. So then Mom decided that her daughter was "attention-seeking." But when Mom again tried reaching out to her daughter with interest, sometimes she was rebuffed but she also was sometimes invited into her daughter's world. Mom was able to show that she was offering attention because she liked spending time and energy with her daughter.

I remember trying to offer my own children my companionship and affection during this stage and being met with the eye roll and a particular tone of "Mom!" And while I could let hugs be accepted or not, their choice, I needed to express my affection and love, so "I love you!" was said with no expectations of a word back and very often there wasn't a response.

Similarly, as a therapist, I can offer my genuine "liking" of a tween client with no expectations but sometimes I see a glimmer in eyes that are searching for acceptance.

"Your relationship assures them that they are not alone on their journey, that you will act in helpful and therapeutic ways to protect them from external and internal threats, and that you want to deeply know their emotional world" (Stewart & Echterling, 2017, p.77).

Chapter 10

UNIQUE CHALLENGES

We all know that there are particular events, unforeseen circumstances and issues present in the social fabric we exist in, that people seek therapy for. My belief is that the mental health field has historically pathologized the client (or patient) for external issues that any human would struggle with. I believe that anxiety and depression, for example, are normal reactions to difficult circumstances much of the time. And humans do the best they can at the time, in difficult situations. And sometimes our coping mechanisms are problematic in themselves, or just fall apart in the face of situations that can seem insurmountable.

I interviewed a few therapists who have developed important skills and practices while creating therapeutic relationships with children during very particular life challenges that these young clients were living through.

Cheryl works with children and families who have experienced domestic violence. Sometimes very small children have witnessed someone beating or raping a parent. And then perhaps they have been part of a difficult escape to safety, leaving belongings and pets behind. Where the family finds shelter can feel strange and overwhelming. The fear is carried with them, into the safe space.

Cheryl makes it completely clear for her young clients that "They don't have to share anything" (Cheryl, personal communication, June 27, 2021). She offers Play-Doh for squishing as she helps explain to the child who she is, and why she's there, and what the confidentiality limits are. They've come out of a time when chaos, not boundaries, defined existence. Setting limits and boundaries gives structure and a sense that the world now has a little order and reliability. I love that she says to them: "You've just been through something scary. Your body might not want to be still." She encourages running in a safe place, and she watches them and praises them for running and not hurting anyone. She has access to a large full-body swing that they can swing on and feel the rhythm of. She literally helps them shake it off and then understand the differences between bodies that feel wild and crazy, and bodies knowing how to find stillness and quiet.

She doesn't expect that children will tell her their experiences in a logical order. Little bits and pieces come out in play or art. Dreamwork might suddenly appear, showing up in art, rich with metaphor. Cheryl is fine with sitting in silence. She might pick up something and start playing with it, which can encourage a child to also find something that they might enjoy or find comfort in.

She lets the children take the lead, in terms of the flow of the talking, when it does happen. If they seem to constrict or tense up with a question or comment, she pulls back, letting them take the lead again. Cheryl is also aware, in the midst of their difficult memories, that sometimes it's important for the therapist to say things like: "You're safe right now where you're at. Feel the table, look around the room and see where you're at. What colors do you see? Do you like the smell of crayons or Play-Doh?" Cheryl emphasized how much play and art happens, perhaps in multiple sessions, before words and stories can be shared. She deeply appreciates how hard and strange it can be for a child to trust a new adult in their life.

While working for this agency, Cheryl has experienced listening to horrifying stories of violence and deep sadness. When we work with children who contain such difficult memories, we need to work extra hard at dealing with what we know, so that we can have our own happy lives. Worksheet #24 is a place to reflect on how you do this, and if this self-care is adequate or not.

WORKSHEET #24

How do you deal with the hardest client stories?

where do you put work stories at the end of the day?

Do you ever have trouble sleeping?

Dreams?

Caitlin has worked with children from several different Pueblos (a Pueblo is a Native American community in New Mexico). Her young clients come to therapy with the same issues as any children, anywhere, and their experience of who adults are is based on the adults in their particular community.

Caitlin is not Native American. I often found myself working with children who were from different racial or cultural backgrounds than mine. I yearned for them to see a therapist who looked like them, and helping the field of mental health become more accessible to all people as a career is an ongoing passion of mine.

> The mental health profession is an elite, privileged institution crafted in such a way as to make entry somewhat daunting. Not only do you need to have the time to undertake a long course of study, something that is not possible for many young people of color, who must often prioritize earning money, supporting their families... (Gil, 2021, p.41)

And until there is more support for all humans to be able to consider entering a career in mental health, and affording the cost of the necessary education, therapists will need to figure out how to connect with those who are somehow unlike them, in authenticity, humbleness and transparency.

Caitlin enjoys offering art materials and sometimes she'll start to make something herself, never afraid of the silence that might be in the room. She never tells children what to create and follows the child's lead, taking time for the relationship to develop.

She intentionally models an appreciation of imagination and fun. She likes to ask silly questions: "If you lived on another planet, what would it look like? It can look like anything you think of" (Caitlin, personal communication, February 25, 2021).

She also finds small things to connect with, noticing backpacks, clothing, light-up sneakers. She notices things about her clients, helping them to feel seen. She shared that some little girls like to dress up to come to therapy. And her clients haven't seemed to see race as a barrier in their relationship. Children have excitedly volunteered information when they have noticed the visual differences between themselves and Caitlin. "Children are not color blind, rather they can notice and feel differences and even comment on those perceived differences. What children don't have when they are very young is a tendency to think negatively about skin color" (Gil, 2021, p.39). I appreciate Caitlin's stance on children's questions. If a child asks her a question about herself or where she's from, she gives them a real answer, often incorporating imagination: "My family came from where leprechauns come from."

Her work with clients often moves out and touches family members. She spoke of a little girl who spotted a miniature building in Caitlin's office that Caitlin had created.

She asked Caitlin to teach her how to build a tiny building. Caitlin showed her how and gave her some simple materials that she took home and shared with her siblings. The young client brought their creation in the next week to show Caitlin. Caitlin and her client decided to walk around outside to find some sticks to use in the creation. Her client took it home again and then the child's father got involved and made some curtains for it. The house became something that Caitlin and her client sat down on the floor together and played with, and during that play, important talking could happen.

I was delighted to talk with another therapist, Brittnee, who believed that it was fine if therapy with her young clients turned into a fun time. I've encountered therapists over the years who somehow didn't think that they were really doing therapy if it became fun.

Brittnee is a child life specialist and art therapist who worked in hospitals with children. She emphasized, in our conversation, that it was important in that setting to define what a safe environment is, and how one can adapt the idea of a safe container for therapy to a hospital room. One of the challenges was that she wasn't sure if she had ever had a session that wasn't interrupted. There seemed to be the sense that art therapy was somewhat trivialized by others, who didn't think twice about interrupting.

Brittnee herself was always careful to "not barge into a room" (Brittnee, personal communication, June 8, 2021). She respected the nature of a patient's space and so she would knock loudly and listen. If invited in she would introduce herself and ask the child's name and pronouns, not relying on the chart but really hearing this from the child. She was clear about her role and what she could do. She wanted to authentically support patients and Brittnee received far more referrals each week than she could possibly respond to. She used developmental and situational needs in order to prioritize, in particular, the older child or teen who was truly navigating existential issues triggered by illness or hospitalization.

When one considers all the staff that children interact with in the hospital, Brittnee was someone who wasn't going to physically hurt them or do procedures that seemed scary. She offered the creation of a relationship based on what the child or teen wanted or needed. "I didn't ignore the medical environment," she stated as she spoke about her relationships with her patients. She helped her patients attach new meanings to medical materials, including sponges, long Q-tips and other items suitable for art making. She also helped clients create a portfolio of their work, within clear plastic pages in a type of journal that they could take home, share with family members or, sadly, the families could take home if the patient died. When working with the Palliative Care Team, the family and patient would have the opportunity to be together while creating art.

Issues surrounding grief, loss and trauma are also held beautifully by two women who work with children and families at an organization created for grieving kids and families. I continue to be moved by the work that Katrina and Roxana do. I also was struck by the flow of ideas and communication between them when I interviewed them. I asked them how they approach the creation of relationships with children who have suffered a loss or death. Katrina spoke first, emphasizing that one needs to be mindful of preparing for the session: "Be in a space of love, loving yourself so that you are able to offer the child loving acceptance" (Katrina, personal communication, July 20, 2021). What is a ritual or a process that you do or can develop in order to be in that space to love yourself and offer loving acceptance? Please use Worksheet #25 to name your own practices.

WORKSHEET #25

what helps you be in a space of loving yourself so you can offer acceptance to others?

Katrina spoke passionately about the need to believe in the power that the child has to heal: "When we believe in them, grief is a natural process. Believe in their knowing." Katrina asks herself: "Am I honoring the magnificent power of this person to heal?" Roxana agreed: "They have what they need to heal. Kids can sense our presence, our nervousness, if we're holding that. They can feel if we trust them" (Roxana, personal communication, July 20, 2021). I appreciate this belief in the person's own sense of themselves and what they need, along with our roles of being present and curious. Katrina referenced the idea of companioning in grief work, a way of working described by Alan D. Wolfelt in his writings: "As a caregiver to mourners, I am a companion, not a 'guide'—which assumes a knowledge to another's soul I cannot claim. Neither am I an expert. To companion our fellow humans means to watch and learn" (Wolfelt, 2016, p.12). I encourage you to seek out his list of 11 tenets of companioning that are found in his book. I appreciate how Katrina and Roxana model their work on his unique understanding of working with grief, shared beautifully here: "Companioning people in grief is therefore not about assessing, analyzing, fixing, or resolving another's grief. Instead it's about being totally present to the mourner—even being a temporary guardian of her soul" (Wolfelt, 2016, p.10).

Roxana spoke about how she spends time getting to know her young clients first, playing with them, helping them to trust her. Both women emphasized to the children that they didn't have to talk; they tell children that they're not trying to get them to open up. (I've worked with so many new therapists who believe that if a child doesn't "open up" in an early session, that they didn't really "do therapy.") Katrina shared that she purposefully avoids asking "How do you feel?", and uses questions carefully.

Both women have plenty of options available so that children have choice and power in the situation. They reassure them of all the things they don't have to do or say. I loved Roxana's story about doing nothing. She was working with a small boy and he just put his head down on the table when he was offered options of things to do. Roxana normalized that sometimes it's okay to do nothing: "I did nothing with him," and she too, put her head down on the table. She described to me how she validates what they're going through: "There's nothing wrong with you," which helps create a sense of safety in their relationship with her.

I think as a therapist thinks about working with children who have experienced grief, we should look at our own family and culture's beliefs about death. Worksheet #26 offers a space to reflect on experiences and traditions connected to death, from your memories. Fear and discomfort, religious beliefs and practices all inform what we bring of ourselves to this topic in our work.

*

WORKSHEET #26

what experiences with death have you had?

_____

_____

_____

_____

what rituals did your family have, traditions about mourning?

_____

_____

_____

_____

_____

what are your spiritual beliefs?

_____

_____

_____

_____

Sometimes we need to be clear about the grief and healing present within our own timeline when we consider this work. Grief doesn't evaporate, but the power of it can be so intense that we can be too vulnerable to sit with it and see grieving clients at the same time. Our own grief can help us be exquisitely sensitive and empathetic, and we might also still be too fragile.

Katrina spoke about the need to share a little about oneself, especially with older kids who want to know about you. She talked about the need to keep humility, be present and stay open. She thinks of this when getting to know a child, "This person is a brand-new mystery," and her boundaries are reflected in how much she chooses to share, while love is the essence of the therapeutic relationship: "Love and boundaries can exist in the same space."

I believe that any therapist might encounter similar issues, whether or not they work in one of these specialized settings. We may very well need to be with and contain many of these same issues in our work with children. All therapists interviewed in this chapter have given their authentic selves in relationships with their clients, to the immense benefit of their clients. I find myself humbly grateful for their good work.

Chapter 11

CHILD CLIENTS SHARE THEIR THOUGHTS

When I was a little girl we lived next door to a wonderful, older couple who we called "Grandma Ruth" and "Grandpa Joseph." My memory of Grandma Ruth especially is held in vivid sensory recollections and specific moments of play. I remember that she trusted me to play with her beautiful Russian nesting dolls. I remember that she let me help make cookies, she taught me to crochet, and she had soap in her bathroom that smelled and looked like rose petals.

So I don't know why I was surprised that these kinds of memories were also held by children who had been to see a therapist. I didn't necessarily hear how seeing a therapist helped them feel better or helped them get through a hard time. I heard about experiences of play, art and games. I heard about a dollhouse that had all kinds of furniture, and different ages and colors of dolls. I heard about glitter. Lots of glitter. I heard about playing Jenga that had questions written on the sides of the wooden pieces. I heard about games they won, and art presents they had made for family members. I heard about 3D creatures that were created with wooden scraps and found objects and the fun battles that they had with them.

A nine-year-old child (not my client) did talk a little about what he remembered about therapy. I invited him to choose a different name to use in the book and he decided on "Isaiah." Isaiah began by talking about the toys and books that one therapist had: "He had my kind of things, like Star Wars Lego and a good Superman book" (Isaiah, personal communication, September 22, 2021).

I asked him if he remembered some other good things about therapy and he said that the therapist "helped him talk to my parents" (Isaiah, personal communication, September 22, 2021) and that he didn't think he was arguing with them so much anymore.

When I asked him if there were things that were hard about going to therapy, he spoke up right away: "It's hard at first to talk about what's going on. It's hard to talk" (Isaiah, personal communication, September 22, 2021). I knew that he'd seen a few therapists due to people leaving or changing jobs within an agency. The transition to a new therapist was definitely hard for him. He said he was really nervous, and it felt hard to get to know a new person.

Isaiah also said that even though he would be nervous, he would consider going back to a therapist if things in life seemed difficult again. I think that's a good thing for therapists to remember: we're helping our young clients understand that therapy is okay. I think that means that they would consider seeing a therapist, if needed, later on in life. Adult clients sometimes wait quite a while to decide to seek therapy; I have to believe that they might go to therapy sooner if they had a good first experience as a child.

Chapter 12

SAYING GOODBYE

The emphasis in this workbook has certainly been on creating healthy and meaningful therapeutic relationships with children. It may seem odd to discuss termination here, but I think that much of how we establish relationships contributes to a more satisfying ending to the relationships for our clients, their adults and ourselves.

Think about the word goodbye. This word can carry so much with it. If we picture goodbye as something contained in our emotional baggage, I think it might take up a lot of space. Most of us have experienced some hard goodbyes in life. Children often have too. Death of pets and people, moves across the planet or the town, people who are partners to a parent who are suddenly not in the family's life anymore. Some children have been taken away from a parent or family member. Some children have been moved repeatedly, without time to understand the circumstances or say goodbye. Take a little time with Worksheet #27 and sit with the word goodbye, and see what surfaces for you. There are therapists who seem as uncomfortable with the concept as their clients may be.

*

WORKSHEET #27

Any baggage around the word "goodbye"?

I like to imagine what a "good" goodbye could look like. If I have developed and maintained a relationship with warmth and authenticity, the closing of it should also be held in that way. The end of our work with a young client can contain so much joy as we reflect on what we did together. If we made art, we can look at it or look at pictures of it. There can be a lot of "Remember that time..." as we summarize the therapeutic journey. I liked to have time with the child alone, and with the child and adult, as we near termination. My deepest hope is that we have some advance warning if termination is happening before we might have suggested it.

Families make some fast decisions, though. Sometimes we don't have a few weeks to prepare, it might just be a few days, which means we have one session to celebrate our client's good work and let them know how much they mean to us.

During a last session I believe in revisiting the hope I held in that initial session, and now add on hope for the future. I like to make art together for each other in the last session. It gives me a chance to write down some words and illustrate them, so that they can be remembered on a tough day, perhaps. It can be a way for me to demonstrate that I really saw, heard and *knew* them as a special human. I won't forget this special human. "Whether we're a preschooler or a young teen, a graduating college senior or a retired person, we human beings all want to know that we're acceptable, that our being alive somehow makes a difference in the lives of others" (Rogers, 2003, p.162).

When you think about your young client, what do you want them to know that you feel and believe about them? These words need to come from our hearts and our brains. "I believe that you are going to keep using all your skills when you get angry, and that you will be able to figure out if you're sad or scared and not really so angry. I know that you know how to say those hard things to your mom now." And the heart response might be more like "I'm going to miss you! You are a kind person and you really know how to make me laugh!"

If our relationship has been genuine, our goodbyes will be too. And the tone of our relationship was established during the very first session. Likewise, the tone of our relationship with the parent or caregiver was also established. It is hoped that they have come to know us as a person who respects them and appreciates the hard work of parenting. We might want to offer some ideas of developmental stages when children, tweens or adolescents sometimes want to revisit therapy. As parents talk about their child, I like to emphasize the positive, strength-base issues in the conversation. John and Rita Sommers-Flanagan use a particular process as they do reflective listening with parents: "we imagine using a bright-orange highlighter to help parents vividly see the words they're using to represent their successes... These reflections intentionally direct parents to look at and *own* their positive efforts, insights, abilities and outcomes" (Sommers-Flanagan & Sommers-Flanagan, 2011, p.181).

These positive conversations with both parents and children reinforce that the credit for progress, improvement, increased peace and happiness goes to the parents and children.

Chapter 13

CONCLUSIONS

I truly appreciated the similar themes that seemed to weave in and out of the conversations with therapists about their work. The first important message from them all seemed to be that children are very different from adults and need an approach in therapy from a softer, more observant place. The pace of therapy is different; therapy with a child won't move forward the same way it can with an adult. There will be time needed to create a safe, trusting relationship before a therapist gets to whatever "the issue" is in conversation. And the issue probably will surface first in play with toys and puppets, art making or playing games.

Each therapist really liked working with children. That was evident in how they spoke about them and how they described their thoughts when working with them. Therapists were curious and strength-based. This is reinforced by Shannon: "When you are with the patient, try to go beyond words. Try to appreciate that person's presence. Is it vital, joyful, and alive? How is the expression of positive affect?" (Shannon, 2013, p.178).

Over and over again I heard therapists and authors refer to the importance of play. And the importance of the therapist to be playful—genuinely engaged in authentic play with their young client. Along with play the idea of following the child's lead seemed to go hand in hand. Observing and following, watching choices and patterns.

A truly humble approach when working with families seemed held with utmost importance. We have to remember that we come to this work with our ideas formed by our own family of origin experiences, which means we may make assumptions about the correctness or superiority of those experiences, or we may still find ourselves acting out of reaction to negative experiences. We need to be skilled at setting aside what we think is a "happy" or "healthy" family, and be open to lots of versions of happy, healthy families that exist in the world. I think of each family as their own unique culture, created from generations of people who created family life the best they could.

I invite you to use the final worksheet, Worksheet #28, to track things that you try and note ideas that you like (and those that you don't), so you have a place to return to for approaches and experiences to engage in.

*

WORKSHEET #28

A place to track your experiences:

Experiences/activities

Ideas to try

The thought I treasure about working with children continues to be the idea of *big hope* for their good futures. Being even a tiny part of helping a child move forward in life with a sense of increased hope or joy has always brought me hope and joy in this work.

References

Altvater, R. (2021). The culture of technology and play therapy. In E. Gil and A.A. Drewes (Eds.), *Cultural issues in play therapy* (2nd Ed.). New York: Guilford.

Freeman, J., Epston, D. & Lobovitz, D. (1997). *Playful approaches to serious problems, narrative therapy with children and their families.* New York: W.W. Norton.

Gil, E. (1991). *The healing power of play, working with abused children.* New York: Guilford.

Gil, E. (2021). *Cultural issues in play therapy* (2nd Ed.). New York: Guilford.

Glasser, H. & Easley, J. (1998). *Transforming the difficult child.* Tucson, AZ: Nurtured Heart Publications.

Graham, P. & Midgley, N. (2020). *So young, so sad, so listen, a parents' guide to depression in children and young people* (3rd Ed.). Cambridge, UK: University Printing House.

Hooper, J. (2012). *What children need to be happy, confident and successful.* London, UK: Jessica Kingsley Publishers.

Malchiodi, A.A. (2020). *Trauma and expressive arts therapy, brain, body, & imagination in the healing process.* New York: Guilford.

Malchiodi, C.A. & Crenshaw, D.A. (2017). *What to do when children clam up in psychotherapy, interventions to facilitate communication.* New York: Guilford.

Oaklander, V. (2007). *Hidden trauma, a map to the child's inner self.* London, UK: Karnac.

O'Neill, P. (2019). *Sometimes I'm anxious.* New York: Sky Pony Press.

Perry, B.D. & Szalavitz, M. (2006). *The boy who was raised as a dog, and other stories from a child psychiatrist's notebook.* New York: Basic Books.

Rogers, F. (1994). *Mister Rogers' playbook: insights and activities for parents and children.* New York: Barnes & Noble.

Rogers, F. (2003). *The world according to Mister Rogers.* New York: Hyperion.

Rogers, F. (2006). *Many ways to say I love you.* New York: Hyperion.

Rubin, J. (2005). *Child art therapy* (3rd. Ed.). Hoboken, NJ: Wiley.

Schroder, D. (2005). *Little windows into art therapy.* London, UK: Jessica Kingsley Publishers.

Shannon, S.M. (2013). *Mental health for the whole child.* New York: W.W. Norton.

Smelser, Q.K. (2021). Exploring gender and sexuality using play therapy. In E. Gil & A.A. Drewes (Eds.), *Cultural issues in play therapy.* New York: Guilford.

Sommers-Flanagan, J. & Sommers-Flanagan, R. (2011). *How to listen so parents will talk & talk so parents will listen.* Hoboken, NJ: Wiley.

Sommers-Flanagan, J. & Sommers-Flanagan, R. (2017). *Clinical interviewing* (6th Ed). Hoboken, NJ: Wiley.

Stewart, A. & Echterling, L.G. (2017). The sound of silence in play therapy. In C.A. Malchiodi & D.A. Crenshaw (Eds.), *What to do when children clam up in psychotherapy, interventions to facilitate communication.* New York: Guilford.

Winnicott, D.W. (1971). *Playing and reality.* New York: Tavistock.

Wolfelt, A.D. (2016). *Counseling skills for companioning the mourner.* Fort Collins, CO: Companion Press.